CARDINAL
POINTS

Mapping
Adelaide's
diversity —
people,
places,
points
of view

**Wakefield
Press**

NEXUS

Multicultural Arts Centre Inc

Wakefield Press
17 Rundle Street
Kent Town
South Australia 5067

First published 2001

Photography by Samantha Oster
Designed by Liz Nicholson, design BITE
Printed and bound by Hyde Park Press

National Library of Australia
Cataloguing-in-publication entry

ISBN 1 86254 565 0

Cardinal Points Project Team
Executive Director – Mirna Heruc
Project Co-ordinator & Curator – Niki Vouis
Oral Historians – Anna Gillam, Michael Lim, and Nikki Marcel
Photography & Image Design – Samantha Oster
Editor – Malcolm Walker

Acknowledgements
Nexus would like to thank Dr Vesna Drapac of the University of Adelaide for her helpful suggestions at the inception of the project, Valeria Ledda for her initial research and George Lewkowicz for his generous assistance and insight with the selection process. Thanks also go to Ian North, Sue Williams and the team at Wakefield Press for their time, encouragement and support. Nexus wishes to thank Elizabeth Sykora and the staff and board members of Nexus for their ongoing support. In particular Nexus would like to applaud the fourteen interviewees who, in the midst of family and work commitments, gave generously of their time and enthusiasm and allowed us to peer momentarily into their lives.

Nexus also wishes to acknowledge and thank the Department of Communications, Information, Technology and the Arts – Centenary of Federation Community Projects Fund for funding this project. Thanks also to Wakefield Press and Ilford Imaging Australia for their generous sponsorship, and to Arts SA and the Australia Council for the Arts for their ongoing support.

CONTENTS

Introduction   4

CHEONG LIEW   5

DIMITRI DALAGIORGOS   8

EDUARDO ABARCA   11

HOSSEIN VALAMANESH   14

IRENE LEIGHTON   17

LUCIA ROSELLA AND NICOLINA BUGEJA   20

RAZAK MOHAMMED   23

SHIRLEY PEISLEY   26

STEPHANIE BURLEY   29

ELTAHIR MALIK   32

TANGI STEEN   35

VILI MILISITS   38

INTRODUCTION

MIRNA HERUC,
Executive
Director

NIKI VOUIS,
Project
Co-ordinator
and Curator

Cardinal Points is a collection of twelve stories, which, together with the accompanying photographs, highlights the rich social diversity brought to the Federal electoral seat of Adelaide by people of different cultural and linguistic backgrounds. A Centenary of Federation Community Project, its aim was to cover a range of professional and personal trajectories through a visual record and oral histories. These paths record not only personal events – a boy's trauma at leaving his dog behind, through to a migrant's shock upon disembarkation during the 1983 Ash Wednesday bush fires – but also explore the contributions made by the interviewees in the fields of politics, business and the arts. *Cardinal Points* does not refer exclusively to geographical origins, rather it is suggestive of another kind of journey, one which encompasses a connection to place, to family, friends, work and play, and to the social landscape that constitutes Australia today.

The Nexus Multicultural Arts Centre conceived *Cardinal Points* as an explorative project producing an image of the electorate beyond the everyday surface. With the project working in three stages, Nexus first drew together a team of oral historians who researched prospective participants, spent time in conversation with them and finally transcribed each interview. The second stage involved compiling and editing the stories. Stage three comprised photographing the participants. Three shots were taken of each person – a portrait, the hands and an object of personal significance – with the images featuring both in the book and in the accompanying exhibition in the Nexus Gallery. To place both images and texts within an electoral context, map references from the Gregory's Street Directory appear on the page giving each its own cardinal point (Adelaide 2001, 49th Edition).

As if to echo the play of relationships between images and texts, the stories contrast and interweave the private and the public realm through the telling of everyday activities, family histories, aspirations, and perceptions of the local community. Stemming principally, but not exclusively, from people of non-English speaking backgrounds, the stories mark the immense cultural changes that have occurred in the decades leading up to Australia's Centenary of Federation. Many of these changes are in part due to the relaxation of exclusionary migration policies and introduction of multicultural social policies. *Cardinal Points* explores what it takes to achieve a sense of pride and belonging in Australian multicultural society, whilst at the same time preserving one's own sense of cultural identity.

On a local level, each story offers an account of life interwoven into the framework of a buzzing and thriving Adelaide Federal Electorate urbanscape: Nediz Restaurant on Hutt Street, the Miss Gladys Sym Choon Gift Store on Rundle Street, the Central Market and one of the city's oldest suburbs, Bowden–Brompton, part of which was once known to locals as 'Little Paris'.

The participants – Eduardo and Yubitza Abarca, Nicolina Bugeja, Stephanie Burley, Dimitri Dalagiorgos, Irene Leighton, Cheong Liew, Eltahir Malik, Vili Milisits, Razak Mohammed, Shirley Peisley, Lucia Rosella, Tangi Steen, and Hossein Valamanesh – contributed generously to *Cardinal Points*. In reading their stories we hope that you will experience the wealth of cultural and linguistic diversity which is now contemporary Australia.

CHEONG LIEW

Cheong Liew is the consultant chef to the Grange Restaurant at the Hilton Hotel, Adelaide. Originally intending to study electronics, he found his passion for cooking was ignited while working at a city restaurant during a summer visit to his brother. In 1975, after working in a variety of situations around Adelaide, he opened the highly acclaimed Nediz restaurant. Cheong is married with four children, and his whole family is now reunited and living in Adelaide.

My father was first-generation Chinese in Malaysia. My grandfather was into tin and rubber. After the war there wasn't much use for those commodities, so my dad sold everything and got into poultry farming with my uncle. We grew up on the farm – we had vegetable gardens, some fish farming, along with banana and papaya plantations – but the family also had its own restaurants. After 1969 the whole family decided to give everything up and move all around the world. Fifteen years later we ended up living here in Adelaide – Mum, Dad, my three brothers and five sisters – although my mum and dad came out through the family reunion program. They've loved this city ever since.

Cooking found me. I was working part time at the Iliad restaurant in Whitmore Square. It had only been open a week when I was asked to help the chef and look after the grill. It was fantastic to be cooking. Everybody appreciated what I was doing and the Greek chef saw that I had a natural talent and offered me books to read. From then on I bought more books, especially on Greek food so that I could understand what he was talking about. Really, I'm a self-taught chef. The thing about being self-taught is you have to try and reason it out for yourself; ensure that your method is actually logical. Whether you are making a soufflé or a curry, you have to analyse it and make simple deductions because you've never cooked that dish before.

Through cooking I really like to understand other people's cultures. On coming to Australia, you wonder, 'Who are the Australians?' What excites me – with all the new people here in Australia – is exploring these cultures and asking: 'How do they think? What do they do in their home? What do they cook in their kitchen?' This intrigues me, still.

Before I came here I didn't know much about Australia. The only thing I knew was that it was English speaking. I thought it would be very European. Later on, I realised it's less European than I first imagined, but I was happy with the Australian character because it's down-to-earth and honest. 'Your shout mate!' – those were the first words I learnt.

Adelaide gave me the space to be revolutionary. We started with a restaurant in Hutt Street, Nediz, in 1975. I met my business partner, Barry Ross, in a colonial Indian restaurant. He said, 'Cheong, why don't we start up something of our own?' In my typical gung-ho style I said, 'Yes!' Nediz was started with absolutely no plan. All we knew was that I would be cooking and Barry would be serving. We didn't discuss what type of restaurant we were going to open, we just went in blank. Every morning we'd go to the East End markets to pick up our ingredients, then over to the Central Market to pick up the fish and meat, and then we'd come back to the restaurant

A:12

ADELAIDE

SOUTH

AUSTRALIA

CENTRE SOUTH

MAP REF: 182

and write up the chalkboard menu for lunch. At that stage I was using some of the dishes from the Greek, Chinese and French restaurants I'd worked at. It was a really mixed style. The response was wonderful. I didn't realise Nediz was so famous until after I left.

Cooking is about the love of fire and the flame. It's an understanding of other cultures. I like to get as close to the temperament of a culture as I can and to feel as if I'm one of them. For example, beef stroganoff – I want to make sure I am cooking stroganoff as if I'm close to that place in Russia where it originated. It's a tartar dish and they don't use tomato sauce, they use mushroom with sour cream and mustard and a touch of dill and one egg. Other than the sour cream everything is like the northern Chinese style of stir-frying. There's a similarity, which is how you relate to those dishes. I want to do a top stroganoff as if you're eating in the best restaurant in Moscow. This was always my dream because I think it's more important to present something that has so much depth, so much history, so much warmth – and so, if I'm cooking a French dish I want the French to recognise that this is the best dish. If I'm cooking Greek, I'm dreaming about the Greek Islands and I would like to be there. Of course, when I started out I couldn't afford to go there, so the only thing I had was dreaming and cooking. But cooking from the heart is like any field of artistic endeavour. You have your own touch, your own temperament. You draw all your senses into it to form something unique, something new. What I display on a dish has to be unique. Ever since I started cooking I've had to be unique.

I'm really proud to be an Australian, especially in Adelaide. We're always the flavour of the month. We never miss a beat here. The countryside is fantastic. Twenty minutes and you're at the beach or in a vineyard in the hills. But the beauty of Adelaide is in its ingredients. If I want to cook Indian, Malaysian, Chinese or Vietnamese, I can go to the Central Market. And there you'll find one of the best food halls in all of Australia. The food is very good, close to a restaurant dish. It's more up-market. I've seen food halls in Melbourne and Sydney and they slop it here and there as though they're just making a buck and couldn't care less what's on the plate. Here people actually care, which I think is wonderful.

I've been here for thirty years. The city has matured an incredible amount. Many of the people who I first met are still here and I see them all the time. And then you have the new arrivals. There are so many styles of social contact you can have. It's absolutely wonderful.

DIMITRI DALAGIORGOS

A:3

ADELAIDE

SOUTH

AUSTRALIA

NORTH WEST

MAP REF: 181

Dimitri Dalagiorgos was the first member of his family to be born in Australia and spent his early years growing up in Coglin Street, Brompton. He started playing music when he was eleven, and then performed in a variety of groups from heavy rock bands to world music and dance ensembles. Dimitri left a conventional job in pursuit of his musical dreams and began making his own instruments. He now has a workshop and gallery on Port Road, Hindmarsh, and makes a variety of stringed lutes from Greece, the Middle East and Asia Minor out of timber such as Huon pine, walnut, spruce, ebony and maple. He has performed at a number of major Australian festivals and continues to play traditional Greek music.

I loved music from when I was very young. When I started playing, I had no interest in Greek music, but my dad tried to push me into it and I ended up playing rock-and-roll. I got into rock in a pretty big way. Greek music didn't get a look in. I was fighting it off. I'd weasel my way out of community things like dances and church and Greek school. I was a bit of a rebel and I didn't know why. I didn't really want to be part of Greek music and the culture, although it was probably more subconscious than conscious. My sister accepted it more than me – that's when I noticed I was born here, rather than in Greece – because I was thinking to myself, 'I'm not really Greek.'

It was confusing for me when I was growing up because I didn't really understand why I had two names. My passport and birth certificate say Peter, but in Greece I'm registered under my baptismal name, Dimitri. I was always a bit afraid to ask why this happened. You think something is being hidden from you. It was ridiculous, but having two cultures as a kid – the Australian lifestyle outside of the house and Greek at home – sets up all sorts of things in your head. I thought that maybe I was adopted. It was a bit weird.

My mum was on her own when she gave birth to me. We lived down in the rural South-East and Dad had to take her to another town because ours didn't have a hospital. Then he was away working for a week. Mum couldn't understand the staff, so the doctor who brought me into the world named me Peter. It stuck. My mum just thought, 'Leave it be.'

Greeks usually baptise before the baby's a year old. During the ceremony the godfather is the important one because he has the right to rename the child, but usually they go with the name the parents have chosen. Everyone thought my godfather would stick with Peter. He changed it to Dimitri. There was this huge confusion. Mum was pretty upset and decided not to call me Dimitri to spite him. When I got older she told me that I had this other name, a real Greek name, unlike Peter.

I started using Dimitri when I began building musical instruments. It just seemed the way to go. I thought, 'I've received the name Dimitri for a reason,' and 'Peter' didn't seem to work for me. It was a big change for me going into a different career. Having a Greek name made the transition more complete.

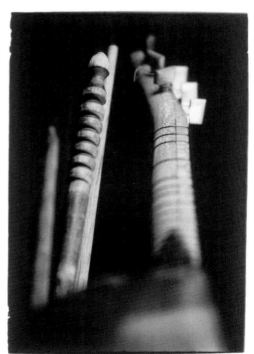

I ended up building my first guitar because I had a pretty boring job and thought, 'There has to be more to life than this!' I'd been toying with the idea of learning to build musical instruments. Having stopped playing rock music there was this emptiness because I wasn't doing anything creative. I like using my hands and instrument making seemed interesting.

I went to a guitar repairer in the city, an older guy, because I thought if anyone knew, he would. I didn't have a clue how to get started. He said, 'The only way is build yourself a guitar.' This light went on in my head. I was on my way to work but drove straight past and ended up in the library with four or five books on guitar making. I was there all day – immersed. I took them home and read them cover to cover. Eventually I found a few people who were involved with it here in Adelaide. It was like opening a door into another world. I was lucky enough to run into someone who had a class once a week. Everyone was making their own instrument and it was very laid back. My first guitar took just over a year to build – it took me on a real journey. From then on I was hooked.

As for my playing, a friend introduced me to *rembetika*, an urban, city blues originating in Athens and Thessaloníki. Ghetto music. It comes mainly from the Greek refugees who were exiled from Turkey and has a bit more of an eastern feel, with these really sweet little melodies. But when you read the lyrics they cover pretty heavy topics – drugs, killings, poverty and, of course, love. It's all about hardship.

I was just blown away by this music. I'd never heard of it before. I wanted to make a *bouzouki* because most *rembetika* music was played on it, and the two things just came together. I ended up making other Greek instruments as well – the *oud*, *zoura* and the *baglama*. I reproduced these instruments because there was nothing readily available here. All we had was the odd picture from which we could measure up and build. We were teaching ourselves. There was no one else here to teach us.

I introduced *rembetika* to Greek players here but they weren't too keen on it. They were playing the folk music that my parents were more familiar with, along with traditional dance music and the seventies' *bouzouki* music from movies like *Zorba the Greek*. I'd grasped Greek music in a different way. From nothing, I developed a remarkably strong connection. *Rembetika* was really important to me. It was a passion. In the sixties, the students in Greece realised that *rembetika* was dying so they dug up all these old players and dragged them into recording studios. Some of it was done really badly, but at least they recorded songs that had never been recorded before. *Rembetika* is still alive because of that.

When I went to Greece for the first time, I became a lot more comfortable with myself. I discovered this other part of me and realised that I could be both a Greek and an Australian – I didn't have that conflict anymore about trying to be one or the other. I'm glad I learnt to speak Greek. I wouldn't want to lose that thread. I'm pleased I picked it up – that my parents pushed it and spoke it at home.

I grew up around Hindmarsh – opened my workshop here on Port Road – and I remember these shops from when I was a little kid and would come and look in the windows. So, I know the area well. As my mum says, 'Even the ants know you here.'

EDUARDO ABARCA

Growing up without a father, Eduardo Abarca struggled to support his family selling crafts, working in restaurants and busking on the streets of Valparaíso, Chile. In 1976 he married Yubitza, a Chilean woman who had grown up in Sydney. They moved to Adelaide in 1988 to reunite with her family and raise their two sons. Regarded as one of Adelaide's original Latino musicians, Eduardo and his band, Sabor Latino, produce the distinctive Latin dance rhythms so popular with audiences. Eduardo works as a store-person during the day.

E:7

ADELAIDE
SOUTH
AUSTRALIA
NORTH WEST
MAP REF: 162

Eduardo I'm a storeman and what I do is receiving, dispatch, packing – using the fork-lift to load and unload. That's it – that's part of every day the same. Before, in Chile, I was a cook working in a restaurant on the weekends, and after, when we came to Australia, I tried to do the same but also I started to play a little 'cafe music' – what they called it many years ago – on the weekend. And then I made a band.

I came to Australia for the family reunion and to see a better future for the kids, not to make music. For me it's not like a business or to look to play, you know, all the time. But what happened was people started to know me more, and so I started to play every weekend. This way I'm getting to be more a musician full-time. But it's not like a business, no, I just want to play music because I started to play guitar when I was fourteen – I was practicing all the time – and learnt to play by ear.

Here, in Australia, we play music from South and Central America – countries like Argentina, Cuba, Mexico, Venezuela, Colombia. Different rhythms. And we make variations. We play folk music from Colombia called *cumbia*. Other rhythms are the *merenge*, folk music from the Dominican Republic, and a new one, the *bomba*, that's from Puerto Rico. We got *salsa* from Cuba. Some of the songs I write, so it's a mixed rhythm. Usually we play simple songs. I remember when my mum listened on an old . . . I don't remember the name . . . ?

Yubitza An old record player that had like a little horn sticking out of it that was the speaker.

Eduardo Yes! It played thick records, very thick, and I remember her putting that on and then playing the song which was 'Moliendo Cafe'. Very old song. Very old one. That is one of the songs that we still play but with a new sound.

Yubitza Good oldies. We just bring them up to be a bit more modern. Eddie's style of music is for all ages – it flows. It doesn't matter if it's a child or a middle aged person, they'll enjoy it just the same. We feel good with those songs because if there's one thing that Eddie always has, it's respect for the music he plays, especially if it's from other musicians. He won't try and do it exactly the same. He'll always take what he feels and adapt it to how he's comfortable playing it, and then that blends into the band and forms a new – not style – but a different sound to the original. What comes across in the music is liveliness, happiness. It's dance music, party music. The songs tell a

11

story in themselves but they're not based on the one thing. It could be anything from a love song to a story about somebody who travelled the world. Music tells many stories. Eddie's found a way of telling old stories in a new way.

Eduardo   In Sabor Latino we've got percussion and congas, timbales, piano, bass, guitar, trumpet. I play the guitar.

Yubitza   We play festivals, restaurants, some clubs. Being a seven-piece band it's not hard to get shows. We recently performed at Elder Park for the Reconciliation Festival. We've gone to Kangaroo Island on more than three occasions.

Eduardo   Sometimes people come, you know, in one of the breaks – old people, fifty or sixty maybe – and they come and shake hands and say, 'Some of your songs I remember from when I was in America.' These people were from the States and they live here now. Or Australians who remember some of the songs from the fifties. They remember the rhythm.

Yubitza   The rhythm is very strong. In Latin America, music is part of the education and culture you're born with – you just have it in you. It's in your blood. You've heard it from your parents, your grandparents. If you walk down a street in Cuba, for example, you can see toddlers banging on a pot with a wooden spoon or just hitting a can to make it sound like a drum. Little kids playing on the street, they'll make a little percussion band out of pots and pans – you name it, they'll be taking it from the kitchen. They'll grab a cheese-grater and a little stick or something, and they'll have you dancing.

Eduardo   When we break or when we finish playing, people come to us – because I'm singing in Spanish, all the songs, just Spanish – and they say, 'I don't know what you sing but it sounds great!' They're dancing, having a good time, and so they feel part of it – even when they don't understand what I'm singing.

Yubitza   It's dance music, you see, the music that Sabor Latino plays. It's not Andean folk music, with panpipes and flutes. It's a mixture of Latin dance rhythms, not music you'd sit and listen to and relax. It gets you up on your feet and lets you have a good time.

Eduardo   We went to see a film called *Buena Vista Social Club*, and I was reading some of the book too. In some of the interviews they're asking the bass player, 'Why did you decide to play bass?' and they say, 'Because my father, he was a bass player.' 'And why did your father play bass?' Because the grandfather, he played bass all his life. It was just like that. The same with the guitar. And singers – coming from generation to generation. Sometimes you reckon he's a good musician, a top musician or singer, because his family was singing, the uncle or the grandmother, but no, he was just listening to his mum everyday when she was cooking, and he likes singing. Music influences me all the time. When I'm happy I like to listen to music and when I'm sad I like to listen to music. When I'm at my work I use a walkman. I work all day with just one ear, and with the other I listen to Latin music. And every hour I put the radio on to listen to the news and then some of the songs, English songs, and I try to listen when they talk too, to understand more, you know, of English. But most of the time I just listen to more music.

HOSSEIN VALAMANESH

Hossein Valamanesh was born in Iran in 1949 and spent most of his childhood in a small town in Baluchistan in the south-east of the country, later returning to Tehran to attend high school and study visual art. In 1973 he immigrated to Australia, and after a short time in Perth, he went and worked among various Aboriginal communities in central Australia. Later he studied at the South Australian School of Art, where he met his wife, Angela. A practicing artist for more than 22 years, he has exhibited extensively in Australia, Asia, Europe and New Zealand. Several of his public art installations are located around Adelaide. One of Australia's most highly respected visual artists, Hossein is represented in Adelaide by the Greenaway Art Gallery.

J:9

ADELAIDE

SOUTH

AUSTRALIA

CENTRE NORTH

MAP REF: 181

Over the years I've made a number of public sculptures or installations in the City of Adelaide. With outside works you have to consider where it's going to be situated. The site is very important. The idea of the work's connection to the earth, of change, of the impermanence of life and passing of time, are all significant factors – all these elements can become part of the work. In a gallery people have more time to contemplate the work on a one-to-one basis, while in public things are much faster. Here you try to create a calmer environment for observing the work. With an outdoor site materials are a whole different ball game. You have to think of public safety – about maintenance and durability.

There's a work of mine behind the Adelaide Convention Centre, *Knocking from the Inside*, which appears to be incomplete. You don't see the whole thing at once, only elements of an imaginary room or place that in some way seem to be falling apart around the viewer. There are two natural-looking rocks at each end and the viewer can begin to imagine lines drawn into the ground, a kind of linearity within the work, which gives it cohesion. For me it's as if there was a place there, maybe, where somebody was trying to open doors, trying to make meaning.

There is a line from a poem by Rumi: 'I have lived on the lip of insanity wanting to know reasons, knocking on a door it opens. I have been knocking from the inside'. It means you're already there but you always think you have to go somewhere else, or that you have to break through. It's this notion of trusting to an inner understanding. Somehow, when the door opens, the artist or the viewer realises that there wasn't any door in the first place, or if there was, that we've placed it there. This is why I have used a theatrical setting incorporating broken columns, as if there is something that has to be demolished for this to be discovered.

In this sense, my sculptural work doesn't come from the western tradition of form and volume and that strong kind of gesture. My interest is in the work not being an object separated from its environment. It must somehow touch the earth – be grounded, and at the same time extend to include the viewer. There is a notion of the theatricality here, so that when a person stands on the work they become part of it. They are not separated as with a more traditional

pedestal object and audience, because that kind of notion suggests the very distinct idea that you are here just to observe, that you're not to get too involved. In this respect I'm inviting physical involvement from the viewer.

With public works a dialogue is set up that is different from work placed in a gallery. To a certain extent these elements I've mentioned, of course, also play a part in my gallery work. An example of this is a gallery piece where I took a Persian carpet, burnt a hole through its centre and documented the process through photographs. That work was made in 1997 for an exhibition entitled *Between Art and Nature*. The image came to me – I don't know – probably over many years. I grew up in Iran. I lived on Persian carpets before having chairs. This was furniture, it was part of our culture, and at the same time these carpets are a form of representation of nature as they're full of flowers and animals. The carpet is a mediation between nature and man because it covers the earth, covers where you're sitting, and so you have this mediation between nature and yourself.

The carpet is taken out into the bush in rural South Australia, my new fire is made at its centre and here is my place – a mediated space containing a representation of a landscape and a real landscape. In a sense such mediation is a form of cultural baggage. I am sitting on this carpet, I've made this new fire, this new life, and this is documented and shown in the form of photographs and then when you come into the gallery and see the carpet, something's missing – there's a black void at its centre.

The work in question is called *Longing/belonging*. Maybe I'm longing a little bit for my country? Am I belonging here or do I belong there, or is it really that I'm longing for here, to be part of this place? And what is this notion of longing? Because, you see, making this piece also coincided with the death of my mother. For me the notion of one's mother includes a sense of the earth, of connection to the earth, and I felt I had lost this really strong connection to my homeland because her presence had always kept me attached to that land. I'm still attached but maybe the umbilical cord has been cut. That's the nature of migration. It's the nature of time, of change – you can't hold onto things. Things are destroyed, things are forgotten. That's the dilemma. But it's a positive thing also, because for me the negative black hole that you see at the centre of the carpet is not a bad thing, it's the possibility of new depths – of the unknown. One is tempted to ask what's inside there and how deep can we travel inside that unknown?

IRENE LEIGHTON

Irene Leighton was born and raised in the western suburbs of Adelaide by politically active parents involved in the trade union and international women's movements. Well known in the Bowden-Brompton area for her local community activism and as a founding member of the Hindmarsh Housing Co-operative, she is a former Alderman of the Hindmarsh City Council and has sat on numerous boards. Her activism has seen her working with a variety of social service organisations, including the Community Legal Service, the Youth Support Scheme and Community Health. Now widowed with three daughters, she continues to assist and participate in local community activities.

In the beginning, my dad was in the IWW, the International Workers of the World. In those days – this was the 1920s – money was so short that when my brother passed away they couldn't afford to bury him. All the men, working men like my father, joined together and helped pay for the funeral. Dad thought he owed them a debt, so by way of saying thank you he joined the IWW.

Anyone who spoke up in those days – and remained a lefty – was considered bad. You had to be very careful. My father started growing vegetables in the back yard, but we had to stop because it made the property more saleable for the owner and we might have lost the house. You know, in order to get rent relief in those days you had to work one day a week pulling weeds on the railway line – that's how government worked in those days.

My mother battled for equality, but equality means different things to different people. Being a person in your own right was always the main thing for her because my father liked to play the patriarch if he could. He agreed women could go out to work – but not *his* wife.

Mum joined International Women's Day. She was secretary for twenty-five years. My father was on the wharves but because labourers were hired on a casual daily basis he became involved with the Unemployed Workers Organisation. During the Depression there was a big meeting at the Waterside Workers Hall. My dad was the chair and they voted to march from Port Adelaide to the city. It was the time of ration tickets and you had to be enrolled at a certain butcher or grocer, you couldn't go to just anyone. It was deemed a beef march because you could only buy mutton and offal.

Mum was always backing Dad up. She had to because he always had people at our house. That's how she got into political activism. Mum's causes were things she considered wrong. For example, they said, 'No guns! Don't give children guns for Christmas,' and she agreed with this because it was encouraging war and there were still strong memories of the First World War where the young men were just cannon fodder.

When I was young I was into the great Australian dream of husband, home and family. I didn't think about politics. I was going to get engaged and married and have children, and, like my mother before me, you're attracted to somebody, they're attracted to you, you both like dancing and what happens? Next thing you're married. Neither Mum nor I ever intended to be political.

0:15

ADELAIDE

SOUTH

AUSTRALIA

NORTH WEST

MAP REF: 163

17

When I became a widow, my brother suggested I move to Bowden, next door to him, which I did. The area was a mix of industrial and residential and my new place was a small one-bedroom cottage, one of six row-cottages. Some Adelaide University students delivered a leaflet saying, 'Be your own landlord! Be a tenant and a landlord at the same time! Save your house!' Houses were being demolished because a freeway was going right through Hindmarsh and Bowden. When people are under threat they ask, 'What can I do about it?'

We started the Hindmarsh Housing Co-operative with these six cottages because it was an industrial area. We had a peppercorn mortgage with the Housing Trust, so we did all the work and everything. They would send someone to the meetings. In those days they really were advisers, they didn't tell you what to do.

The Housing Trust purchased the land at the back of us so we could expand but, bless me if it wasn't contaminated from industrial use in the early days by Browns Metals. In those days it wasn't thought of as wrong to fill up the pug holes with rubbish. Nowadays we know we have to be careful of the environment.

Hindmarsh Housing Co-op had a real social mix in its tenants. We had the old, the young, married and single, and we said, 'What makes a community?' because in our area the people were divided into two sections – home owners and those who rented. There were so many people in Bowden that it was known as 'Little Paris'. Everybody knew everybody else and protected each other. The threat of the freeway really drew people together.

On the freeway issue, Council would blame State Government and vice versa. In order to decide which body was actually causing the problems, I ended up becoming a councillor, which would have been quite horrific if it wasn't for the support I got from locals convincing me I was doing the right thing. It was nothing for sixty people to turn up to a Hindmarsh Residents' meeting. I was there for the residents really, as their representative. I couldn't have done it on my own.

We could always attract the media down here. When the Remand Centre was proposed for Hindmarsh, the man in the street, your ordinary resident, was worried. We didn't feel we could suggest it be put somewhere else, another suburb, because that was simply loading the problem onto somebody else. We started a tent city in the middle of Port Road in protest. They couldn't toss us off because it was crown land. So what I did – because I'm not an early morning person, I like staying up late – I took my caravan down onto the site at night, so that when the demolition workers came at daybreak we could tell them, 'Go and phone your union, the block's black-listed.' We started a second tent city, right there on the proposed Remand Centre site.

Over the years the Hindmarsh Residents have been involved in many similar social justice issues, voicing people's right to continue living in their own homes in the Bowden-Brompton area, whatever their financial or social status. And of course, the freeway was not built, which helped industry as well as the residents.

At the moment a group of us are getting a script together to do a play about the Bowden-Brompton area. It's about – although it's not biographical – an old woman who's likely to lose her house because her son-in-law wants to pinch it off her so he can sell it to the industrialists, that sort of thing. We're not finished yet. I don't think I'll be up front very much but I don't mind helping. But then we can't all be stars.

LUCIA ROSELLA AND NICOLINA BUGEJA

In 1956, one year after her arrival, Lucia Rosella opened a pizza bar in the Central Market. Lucia's is now the oldest surviving Italian pizza bar and cafe in Adelaide. Born and raised on a small farm in Pago Veiano, Italy, with her four sisters and brother, Lucia met her husband, Pasquale, on his return to Italy after he had been a prisoner of war in Victoria. After their marriage, Pasquale realised his dream to return to Australia. Lucia and their children joined him two-and-a-half years later. Lucia's Cafe is now managed by her daughters, Nicolina Bugeja and Maria Rosella. However, Lucia still makes her special tomato sauce.

Lucia Rosella

My husband, Pasquale, had fallen in love with Australia when he was an Italian prisoner of war. I didn't like it in the beginning because I couldn't speak English – people would say good morning but I couldn't answer back. I wanted to earn some money to help my husband but I couldn't because when I looked for a job they would say, 'Come back when you've learnt to speak English.' Then, one day, my Australian next-door neighbour smelt my cooking and said, 'Lucia, what are you cooking?' I couldn't explain it to her, so I gave her a taste. She loved it. It was a pizza. She kept saying, 'Start up a pizza bar! Start up a pizza bar!' That was in 1957. I found a little place in the market and I said, 'That's the one for me.'

It wasn't a very big place. I served pizza, spaghetti, cakes and sandwiches. Lots of people used to come in after the football for a pizza. They all enjoyed it and some wanted to cook it at home. That made me very happy because I enjoy my food and I like everybody else to enjoy it too. And I love to serve people. Now there is a pizza bar on every corner people like it so much.

In those days people didn't drink much coffee. People drank a lot of chicken soup and Bonox and chocolate. So, I used to put a percolator on the stove and make just a couple of cups at a time, and when I finished one pot I'd make another. People would ask what the coffee was like and I'd say, 'You'll have to try it for yourself.' If it was too strong, I'd just put more milk in it. You have to be a little bit clever to select the coffee beans and when you've mixed the coffee, you have to try it first. If you like it, everybody will like it – if you don't like it, nobody will. After trying my coffee some people said, 'I'll never drink tea anymore, just coffee.'

But it was hard working as a woman in those days. People would say, 'Why don't you stay at home?' And I'd say, 'It's all right for you, you were born in Australia. You have money. I need to work and I want to help my husband so we can carry the load together.' Pasquale had another job. When he finished working, he'd come and help me at night. So did my children. I'd bring them with me in the morning and make sure they had a good breakfast, then they'd go to school. They'd come back later, I'd cook them dinner and they'd help me in the pizza bar.

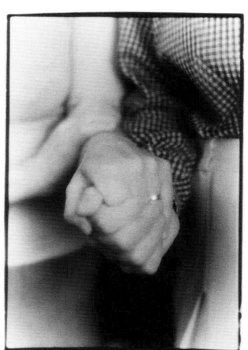

Now my daughters have taken over. I just come in to help in the kitchen three days a week but they still ask my advice. They come home and say, 'Mama, can we do this?' and 'Can we do that?' and I say, 'Yes, yes!'

I'm Australian – my papers are Australian – but my blood is Italian.

Nicolina Bugeja

As a kid I definitely wanted to be Australian. I had to be Australian, no matter what and so a lot of my Italian language was lost. At some stage as a teenager I started to think that I really should be Italian. By then my grandparents were here, my aunties and uncles, and I realised I had this community that I liked. Suddenly, I enjoyed being Italian.

I've got very fond memories of this place – Lucia's Pizza Bar. It's been home for Maria and I since we were kids. We'd come here after school, have our meals here, do our homework. Even when we couldn't reach the sink, we'd stand on a little box so we could help Mum with the dishes. Growing up in the market has been absolutely fantastic. It's a community, like a piazza in Italy where people meet. As a girl, I used to think that people came from all over Adelaide just to use the market as a meeting place. It has such a diversity of people. I've met so many different people from all walks of life in our shop.

People are surprised that it is still called Lucia's Pizza Bar. They think it's a coffee shop. It started out as a pizza bar but now coffee's the biggest seller.

We've been using the same blend of coffee that Mum and Dad mixed all those years ago. They kept tasting different coffees until they came up with the right blend, which is very important, but then so is the person making the coffee. You have to understand coffee – the way people drink coffee and the way Italians drink coffee.

My grandmother used to give us coffee with lots of sugar and when I had children she did exactly the same thing for them – little black coffees with sugar. My children drank it as young as four and now they are all coffee drinkers, but not excessively. They have one or two a day. You just start to appreciate it and learn to know what a good and a bad coffee is.

There are trends too. Cappuccino was the go for so many years, and then all of a sudden somebody came up with *caffélatte* in Melbourne and that was the trend, and more recently we've had the *macchiato*. People say, 'Do you have such a thing as a *macchiato*?' A *macchiato*, to me, just means a coffee stained with milk. And now there is an even newer one still – a shot of expresso coffee with a dollop of ice-cream in it called an *affogato*, which means you suffocate the coffee. It's beautiful, especially in summer.

In Italy coffee is still the rage – the short black. You can have a cappuccino in the morning, up until midday anyway, and after that they sort of look at you as if you're a bit strange. They think you're an *Americano* or something, someone who knows nothing about coffee, and so it doesn't matter how they give it to you. It could be a really bad one.

I was in Italy recently for three-and-a-half weeks with my daughter. We went to Venice, then to Florence and down to Rome. It was wonderful. It was winter and there were no tourists. When I go back to Italy I know that I'm Italian but then again I'm very much Australian too. It's very hard for me. It's strange because over there in Italy I'm not Italian, and here I am Australian but I'm Italian at the same time.

RAZAK MOHAMMED

After working for six years as a builder in his home town in Malaysia, Razak Mohammed came to Australia in 1981 to study. He soon quit and began sewing clothes to sell at the Paddington Market in Sydney. Two years later he came to Adelaide for a party and liked the people so much he moved here permanently. Self-trained in all facets of fashion design and considered avant-garde at the time, his name is now synonymous with the Miss Gladys Sym Choon boutique on Rundle Street. In 1986 Razak's visa expired and he was obliged to return to Malaysia temporarily where he worked for two years in visual merchandising and fashion styling. His subsequent return to Miss Gladys Sym Choon and the development of his successful labels Razak, Milk and Bit, has led to international recognition.

D:10

ADELAIDE
SOUTH
AUSTRALIA
CENTRE EAST
MAP REF: 182

I grew up in Malacca, Malaysia. Our house was in a poor area smack in the middle of the city – open sewers, quite grubby, but actually incredibly multicultural. We lived on Temple Street and directly opposite us was a Chinese temple and then just a hop, skip and a jump away there was a mosque. Next to the mosque was an Indian temple, and right alongside that there was a Sikh temple. It was very colourful. Generally in Asia, if you go to a market, any night market or wet market, you see colour – the clothes people are wearing, the products they're selling – colour everywhere.

I think a lot about colour. I suppose because of my mother and her sense of colour. God, I always remember how gorgeous Mum looked! She'd wear this purple lace with gold thread all over it for her *kabaya*, which is a traditional, fitted number, and then she'd wear, say – a yellow corset. Then she'd wear the totally weirdest combination in her sarong. It clashed but looked amazing! Mum always manages to look the best. It's the way she puts her colours together. But you know, there are still a lot of problems with people readily accepting colours in retail and in the fashion industry generally. Everyone pushes for colour, then you go to a fashion show and all the fashion editors are wearing black. The thing I noticed most when I came to Australia was the lack of colour. Everything was grey and drab, there was very little colour.

I came to Sydney to do the final two years of a Bachelor of Science in building. I did one year, loathed it, and pulled out. I never thought about what was going to happen, I just gave it away. Then my scholarship got pulled. I had no money whatsoever. It was funny though because my flat-mate and I found a sewing machine in the basement and we started fluffing around with it. Started sewing. I suppose Mum had always sewn, and so I knew how to work the machine and we started making things. We got a stall in Paddington Market and sold everything we made. Three weeks later I thought, 'I can do better than this,' so I started making quite lavish garments. This was the eighties, remember. You could just do anything – be as creative as you wanted. And I did. I started selling to a shop in Double Bay. That's how it started.

Eventually I came to Adelaide. I brought all these pieces where I'd treated the cloth like

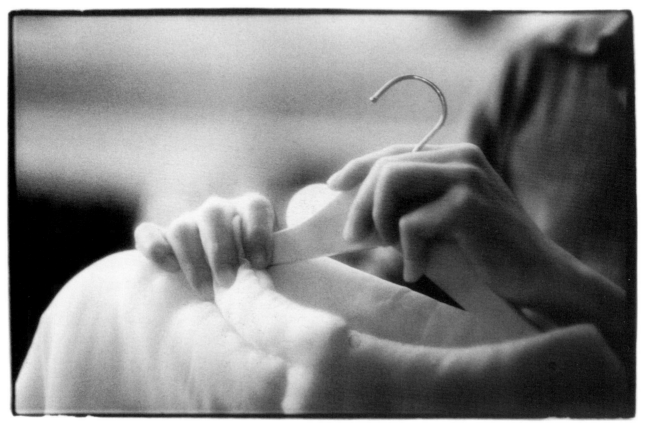

origami. I couldn't sell them here. Too avant-garde. Someone said, 'There's a competition on in a few weeks' time. Why don't you enter these garments?' I remember being skint. Some friends pooled some money and took me along on the night itself – it was the Lady Mayoress Competition – and as I recall, I didn't drink at that stage, so within half an hour I was so pissed! Anyway, I remember going up to the stage three or four times because I won every section, plus the overall award.

We opened a shop, Apparallel, just across the road from the Sym Choon China Gift Store. The 'Miss Gladys Sym Choon' sign was still up, even though Gladys had been married for over fifty years. Anyway, we were across the road eyeing off this shop which kind of reminded me of home, when Gladys' daughter, Mei Ling, decided running the business was a chore and let the shop go. There were six other businesses vying for the place and we got it. I think probably because we asked if we could keep the name. They sold the original sign to us for one hundred dollars and that was that.

Gladys Sym Choon sold the best stuff out of Asia. When no one could enter China she went four times a year and brought back things you just couldn't get in Australia then, everything from Chinese chequers to jade, from lingerie to camphor chests. The windows, which have now made it onto the heritage list, were chock-a-block with amazing things. It was a memorable shop. We still get calls after sixteen years – women ringing up for a placemat or something to match a set they bought thirty years ago. It was the best shop. Some of the stock was fifty years old. We met her many, many times and we always tried to follow her guiding principle, which was to find the very best. You somehow feel that her spirit's still in the shop. It's scary sometimes!

One day, after I'd been in Adelaide for a while, there was a knock on the door, and I can't remember his name, but he's definitely 'Mr Not-nice-guy' and he said, 'Are you Razak?'

'Yes,' I replied.

'You're an illegal immigrant.'

I said, 'Well, I just didn't renew my visa.'

He was from the Immigration Department. After I won the Lady Mayoress Competition I was interviewed in the newspapers several times which is how they must have found me. Mr Not-nice-guy didn't throw me in gaol, thank God, they usually do. He interviewed me for three hours and let me go. It went to court and we almost won because after the competition I got terrific references from the likes of the Lady Mayoress – references from the right people, I suppose. The judge took half an hour to read through them all, and my lawyer, Rose, from Legal Aid, she was saying, 'We're in! We're in!' She was all excited but in the end I was guilty and that was it. I went back to Malaysia. I didn't mind really. It was quite fun being back home.

Now when my brothers visit, we have conversations about me being Australian – because I do identify myself as Australian – but I just can't think the way they do any more. They think that I'm too liberated, too Australian and westernised. They accuse me of such things. But the thing about Australia is that you can actually think and speak for yourself.

SHIRLEY PEISLEY

Shirley Peisley, a Ngarrindjeri elder, was raised in Kingston, South Australia. On moving to Adelaide she completed a secretarial course and worked as a telephonist and secretary. Shirley's employment at the Aboriginal Friends Association immersed her in the Aboriginal Rights Movement, including the 1967 Referendum Campaign to recognise Aboriginal people in the national census. The first Aboriginal probationary officer in the Department of Social Welfare, she is now 'retired', although she still works as the director of the Otherway Centre, as well as being a member of the Reconciliation Council, the Centenary of Federation Committee, and a new body called Reconciliation Australia.

D:11

ADELAIDE

SOUTH

AUSTRALIA

CENTRE EAST

MAP REF: 182

I'm a South-Eastern girl. My grandparents raised me around Kingston during the forties. My grandmother, who grew up on the Pt McLeay (Raukkan) Mission, had strong Christian as well as traditional spiritual values. She felt as happy going to church as she did showing the townspeople how to weave baskets or make feathered flowers from the pelican, her totem. Grandfather tanned animal skins and made beautiful possum-skin rugs, but he also used to invite the local policeman over for a conversation. I grew up with a good knowledge of bush food and medicines and knowing where the springs were. My life was full of cultural riches but I also went to school and did well, becoming school captain and head prefect. I didn't know I was any different. I didn't notice that there might have been prejudice. I knew about racism – my mother told stories about getting jobs and then being told later, 'We can't keep you on because people object to a black woman having this job, so we'll have to ask you to leave. Your work's excellent and we'd like you to stay, but business is business.' I guess I never thought it applied to me.

The year I moved to Adelaide, 1958 or 59, was enlightening – I was nearly arrested for being in the company of a white male. A few of us girls, all students, went off for a Sunday ride in two or three cars and grabbed a hamburger at the beach. I was sitting in the car with my friend, having the meal, when three police cars pulled up and the officers yanked my friend out of the car. We just sat there with our mouths open while these three burly policemen asked me who I was. We'd always been encouraged to be straightforward when questioned by people in authority, so I simply told them that I was an Aboriginal. They asked if I had my exemption on me. I had no idea what they were talking about and asked what an exemption was. Apparently my friend and I could have been charged for consorting. I didn't even know what 'consorting' meant. They explained that Aboriginals, unless exempted, and whites were forbidden from socialising. The Aboriginal Protection Act prevented Aboriginal people from doing all sorts of things unless they had been exempted. And the exemption, which was like a little passport, had to be carried on you if you went into a hotel, were counted on the census, or if you voted. Put simply, it allowed you to call yourself white. So, for many Aboriginal people 'exemption' was a dirty word; if you had one, you were in denial about who you were. It even prevented you from mixing with other Aboriginal people unless they had exemptions.

26

Fortunately I had the foresight to say to the policemen, 'Look, I'm going to the Aboriginal Affairs Department in the city.' We were a respectable family and I hadn't been told about exemptions or consorting. It was not only distressing but also distasteful to know that I didn't have the right to mix. Throughout my school years I'd been mixing with whites; at one stage I was the only Aboriginal in high school. I wouldn't have been able to mix with anyone!

We found out later at the Chief Protector's Office that I was in fact exempted from the Aboriginal Act. That was the first time I actually heard that I was exempted. This was 1960 and my mother was horrified. We hadn't been consulted; we hadn't given our permission. Somebody had just assumed that it was what we would have wanted. It reeked of apartheid. A lot of legislation that had been enacted here was very similar to legislation that had been taken from Queensland to South Africa to establish the apartheid regime there.

In 1967 I became very involved in the referendum campaign – this was to change the constitution so that Aboriginal people would be included in the national census – which gave me a taste for what was happening all around Australia. Prior to the referendum it wasn't very easy for Aboriginal people to gather and talk about the terrible things that were happening in their lives. Public meetings were illegal. People were arrested.

We were coming out of the protection era. I remember my first meeting in Canberra with the Federal Council for Aboriginal and Torres Straight Islanders. I heard the most incredible stories. People were being encouraged to meet and talk about what life was like as an Aboriginal. Someone who comes to mind is Charles Perkins. He was a young man when I first came to Adelaide. What a great friend and role model he was. Everybody looked up to him because he was the first Aboriginal graduate. He was playing sport at an international level but still wasn't allowed to go into a hotel here in Adelaide and drink legally.

It was an amazing part of my life, thinking that for Aboriginal people there was one way to go and that was up. Not to move away from the things that were important, but to understand and appreciate that to bring about any change you needed to accept responsibility, you needed to accept leadership, and you needed to get it right.

I think a lot of Indigenous people need to come around to thinking about being called Australian. It hasn't been a term that people have felt very comfortable with. We've been living in this country without being given full acknowledgment of citizenship. Citizenship only came to us thirty-four years ago. When migrants come to this country they are encouraged to remember their past even if they've endured war or exile. We acknowledge their past and celebrate their culture. Look at Glendi, Carnivale, the Schutzenfest – what a wonderful celebration! Indigenous Australians need to be able to do this too. If you feel that there is a place that you can create for yourself in this country and you haven't been marginalised and separated and divided – that's when you want to be part of the country and have ownership.

There's a lot of work to be done to encourage Aboriginal people to feel that they are Australians and that means that they need to be written into the constitution. It needs to be recognised that we were the first nations, that we had our languages, our culture, that we had our music, song and dance, because it's not just our heritage – it's our legacy and the heritage of all Australians. When that happens we will see all Aboriginal and Islander people in this country really feeling that they are Australians.

STEPHANIE BURLEY

Stephanie Burley remembers her voyage to Australia as being like a holiday cruise where there was no school, only organised play with the other children. On arrival in Adelaide under the 'ten-pound' scheme, her family was housed first in a hostel located where the Festival Theatre now stands and later at the Gepps Cross Hostel, where they spent five years. From an early age Stephanie knew she wanted to be a teacher and subsequently taught at Salisbury High, Salesian College and Wilderness School, before completing a Masters degree in the history of education at Adelaide University where she now lectures in teaching curriculum and methodology.

On finishing university I was posted to Salisbury High School for three years full-time, after which I became pregnant and took about six months off. Salesian College, a Catholic school at Brooklyn Park, needed a part-time history teacher for years eleven and twelve, which was brilliant for me because I loved my teaching but also wanted to be at home with my children. The school had a handful of supposedly difficult youths, but I found them really great.

After I had my third child I remember a nun came into my hospital room and said, 'You have some visitors, Mrs Burley, although I'm not sure that you will want to see them.' I said to let them in and the sister replied, 'Oh, I'm not sure, they're very . . . well, they're louts.' In came half a dozen of my students – big, big lads, you know, with knuckle-dusters and black leather jackets and big boots – the whole bit. It had been obvious to them that I was going to have a baby and they must have seen the birth notice in the paper or something. They stood at the end of my bed chatting away, and then one of them sort of checked to see that nobody was looking and pulled these tiny little booties from his jacket, stuck them at the end of the bed and said, 'They're for the baby.' Then on they went with the conversation. Supposedly they were toughs, but they weren't, they were lovely kids.

We came out under the 'ten-pound' scheme from Glasgow. My father was a general and psychiatric nurse. In Scotland my mother had stayed at home, as was traditional in those days. She suffered from arthritis – rheumatoid and osteo-arthritis – and was advised to shift to a warmer climate because she'd end up in a wheelchair if she didn't.

I was six when we came out here. My parents really wanted me to go to a Catholic school because that was the system in Britain – Catholic children went to Catholic schools. The nearest one to the Gepps Cross Hostel was run by the sisters of Our Lady of the Sacred Heart at Kilburn. I used to catch the tram with some other children from the hostel and we'd walk to school together. For a couple of years I attended a Catholic primary school that opened close to the hostel, but my parents weren't entirely happy and they sent me to St Dominic's over at North Adelaide. That school had a very religious atmosphere. There was the chapel, the cloisters, and even as a child you knew there was something very spiritual about the place. Everything was centred around prayer, teaching, the students and their families, and at that stage the sisters still wore the full

B:8

ADELAIDE

SOUTH

AUSTRALIA

CENTRE NORTH

MAP REF: 182

CHAPEL, CLOISTER & CLASSROOM
REFLECTIONS OF THE DOMINICAN SISTERS
OF NORTH ADELAIDE

STEPHANIE BURLEY
KATHERINE PEACOCK

regalia and they had a dignity that came with it. As a child those things make an impression, you're immersed in it all. They really did care for you. It didn't seem to be quite as strict as some other people's memories of Catholic girls' school – à la *Brides of Christ*, that sort of thing. I mean, you got into trouble, you got told off, but I don't recollect – apart from one nun who rapped us over the knuckles with a ruler – any physical punishment.

For my parents the religious focus was considerable, but for my father in particular, education was very important. He would often say, 'I haven't got any money to leave you but if I make sure that you have a good education you'll never be without, you'll always have something to fall back on.' Both my parents wanted me to have the best education. It was very clear to me that they hoped I would go to university, and they struggled and sacrificed to make sure of that, because it was a fee-paying school – not a really expensive fee-paying school, but they often found it hard to pay the term accounts.

I happily signed an agreement to get into university – the bond to go wherever the Education Department sent me after I finished. I thought it was a wonderful scheme. I doubt I would have got to university otherwise, because at that time they had up-front fees and my parents couldn't afford them. It really was the only way for me to get a degree and become a teacher, which was what I'd always wanted.

I taught at Wilderness School for seven years. Eventually, I felt I wanted another challenge – I didn't want to go into administration, or become a principal or a deputy principal – and I saw a job advertised for a tutor at Adelaide University. No security, but a six-year contract. But you had to work towards a higher degree. I got it and was thrilled because I could still remain in teaching – I was simply teaching prospective teachers.

My husband has been crucial in these endeavours, supporting and encouraging me. I'm also very grateful that my parents came to this country. When I became a lecturer at Adelaide University, I took them for lunch at the staff club, and it was ironic, my father, who had particularly encouraged me, couldn't really believe that I was now a lecturer in this place. He'd worked out I'd be a teacher, that I'd get a university education, but not that I'd become a lecturer. He was very proud but also a bit taken aback. Yet my mother just accepted it as the logical next step. She's been a wonderful role model for me in all the important things in my life.

I feel a loyalty to both Australia and Scotland, but if the crunch comes, if there's a match between Australia and Scotland, I'd go for Australia. I have strong ties to Scotland and I think it's one of the really positive things about this country – I don't believe that allowing dual nationalities and dual loyalties is divisive. Maybe in some instances where people bring the politics from their former country with them and then demonstrate or riot, but to me that's very small-scale stuff within the breadth of things. I think overall this country allows for that divergence, that diversity. As a nation we acknowledge that people have differing loyalties, and we trust that they'll recognise that they have rights and responsibilities as well.

ELTAHIR MALIK

J:11

ADELAIDE

SOUTH

AUSTRALIA

NORTH

MAP REF: 163

The eighth of nine children, Eltahir Malik grew up in a mud-brick house in the Sudanese city of Bhari. He studied engineering in Greece and worked in Libya before marrying Anne, an Australian he met in Greece in 1981. They returned to Adelaide in 1983 and now have four children. Eltahir opened his first restaurant in 1984 and now runs Babanusa on Prospect Road, which incorporates music and traditional crafts as well as food. He performs regularly with local and inter-state bands and is an active soccer player and trainer.

Right from the beginning I've had a certain kind of energy, like electrons – they move, they don't stay in one place. When we were little kids, we were always into music and dancing, and so when I first went to school it felt like hell because I had to sit in the one spot all day. I wasn't used to that type of restriction. I remember for nearly two months I ran away from school. I felt as though my freedom had been taken away from me. I still have that energy. I have to move. Which is why after high school I went to study civil engineering in Greece.

There are large Greek communities in Sudan – we mixed with Greeks, played sport with them and studied Greek history – so I decided that I had better go and find out about all these old European civilisations. Greece is very different – another way of life from the Sudan. I had a one-way ticket, very little money and there was no way I could go back home. It was a bizarre experience. Imagine going to a new country and you have no way of getting home, you don't know the language, you don't know anybody . . . boom! . . . you're lost, as if you were dropped into the sea. I had to look for a job before I had time to learn the Greek language. The very first words I learnt were *ehettè thoulià* which means, 'Do you have work?'

After the civil engineering course I couldn't wait to escape from that profession because you know sometimes you get a wish or desire but you don't know how it will finish, and when it finishes, you realise it wasn't the thing you were looking for. Engineering seemed suited to Greek culture and the way they live but in my culture it's a bit different. In Africa my house has only one door and a little window, but European-style housing is complicated – big windows, lots of glass. It's said they have these windows to bring the outside, inside. In Africa we don't bring the outside inside, we just go outside, because the environment, nature, is very much part of our lives and so we don't need to bring it inside.

I married when I was in Greece. My wife is from Adelaide. Anne came to my flat one day with another friend. I didn't have time to chase girls. I wasn't even thinking of marriage but some-thing inside was pushing me, saying this is the type of person I am looking for. We have four kids now and have been together since 1980. At the time, I never thought I'd come here. Australia was the last thing on my mind.

I arrived in Adelaide on a very hot, dusty day. One of the reasons I'd left Sudan was the heat – often there's a fine dust that comes in everywhere – because weather like that is not for human beings. I had to get out of there. So when I came here I thought, 'I'm back to square one.' It was a shock because I never thought I'd see this dust again. That was Ash Wednesday, 1983.

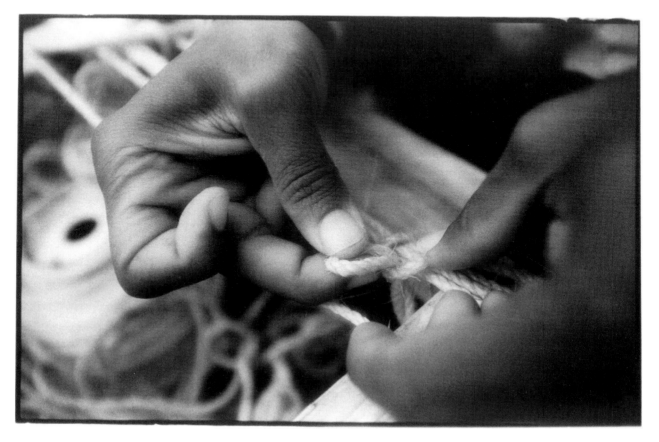

I started drawing, doing illustrations here in Australia. In Sudan – when I ran away from school – I would go and draw. If I look at a face, I can go away and draw it without seeing the person again. I remember a teacher took me to the headmaster to show him my drawing. The headmaster said, 'You should go to the art college.' The words 'art college' were too big for my head. I didn't understand what he was talking about. I couldn't see the value of it at that age. I just wanted to get out of that office because I didn't like teachers.

Coming to Australia, I thought, 'I have to get back to my culture and the way we do things.' In Sudan, if you visit a household and they live far away from you, the whole family goes outside to say goodbye, but it's the one who goes away who fades, who becomes ghostly and disappears. Drawing is a way of depicting my culture, that way of life, and stopping it from fading, becoming ghostly.

I weave, as well. And make beds, which is a very old, traditional craft. My father made beds when I was little and I would watch him – we learn by watching – so, I said, 'Right, I'll make one.' They're not a hammock, but a proper bed with four legs and a frame and a cotton mattress on top, although like a hammock they're suited to the hot areas because they're vented to allow air to come in from the sides. It was interesting because I partially remembered the construction process but couldn't remember how to start. At that time my father had passed away, so there was no way I could write and ask how to begin. Two years later I met a Sudanese cultural researcher at our restaurant and he said to me, 'I know how to do the weaving.' I grabbed a frame and he showed me the start. It was very simple at the beginning. From that I started making the beds and now my kids all have one.

Everything's becoming materialistic. People get very upset over their possessions. Australia's very different from where I grew up. Here capitalism over-emphasises the material and the majority of people are much too materialistic. For me, if you're too materialistic your spirit is finished, because you know, gold, diamonds, bricks, dirt, they're all the same to me. Nature has put the dirt on top and the diamonds deep under the ground, and there's a reason for this. People don't fight over the dirt – they fight over the diamonds. That's why they're kept away from us. And we should leave it that way.

TANGI STEEN

From the Pacific Island of Tonga, Tangi Steen's intellectual prowess led her first to Fiji and then on to Adelaide in 1978. Awarded a scholarship to study Mathematical Sciences, she was one of a small number of women to complete their degrees within the then male dominated mathematics faculty of Adelaide University. After her marriage, Tangi returned to Tonga and worked as a teacher, while her husband, Greg, cared for their twins. Tangi is now in the final stages of completing her PhD at the University of South Australia.

H:10

ADELAIDE
SOUTH
AUSTRALIA
CENTRE WEST
MAP REF: 181

The first thing I noticed about Australia was the time difference. I didn't know about the different time zones. I'd been travelling around the Pacific where all the times are the same. Leaving Sydney for Adelaide I was in a panic because I thought, 'Where's the driver to take me to the airport?' I was fretting, so I rang a taxi, got myself to the airport, checked in and they said, 'Your flight isn't for another two hours.' My driver, who was supposed to pick me up from the hotel, was also panicking because I'd left already.

After I won a scholarship in Mathematical Sciences to study at Adelaide University, I stayed at St Ann's College for two years. It was a nightmare just finding my way around. Adelaide's huge compared to Suva or the Tongan capital, Nuku'alofa. Distance in Tonga and Fiji is very different. Someone may ask, 'Can you go and get that?' and you'll walk because it's only down the road. When I read the street directory here, I had the concept of distance as being only the next street down, not a whole block. My sense of timing was shocking because it took much longer to walk than I anticipated.

When I arrived I was twenty-three and still dependent on my extended family environment – complying with the norm, what everybody else was doing or wearing. In Adelaide people were sitting next to each other on the lawns kissing and holding hands. You're not supposed to do that in public in Tonga. I thought, 'This is a whole new world. I have to establish a new identity,' but I'd hardly made a decision on my own before. There were so many choices. Even a simple thing like buying a biro at the uni shop was confusing because there was a whole rack and I'd think, 'Just give me one biro!' All of a sudden there were all these options. I was fearful of choosing and doubtful about whether it was really the right choice. There were no Tongans to tell me what to do. I was lost, totally lost.

I found for the first time that it was all right to have your own views about things – political views – and it just amazed me what people were saying publicly about politicians. I was thinking, 'These Australians are very rude, they're calling their politicians bastards.' It's only when you look at it in context, how the Australian government works and how the concept of authority is treated, that you start to understand. People question things because they have the right to question. In Tonga, while you have freedom of speech in your home, you cannot publicly say things like, 'The King's not doing the right thing by the people.' The freedom to speak freely, to express an opinion, is something I appreciate about Australian culture. People can express themselves freely here – sometimes too freely.

A question that crops up occasionally is, 'Would it be difficult to go back home to live?' In Tonga my family were being treated differently because I married a *palangi* – a white person – so there would be some invitations for me only and some for both of us. Some people were more at ease if only I attended. My husband had to see a lot of things from my perspective when we were in Tonga. Now people say I'm more Australian than my husband.

There's good and bad about going back. I'd be with my family – there are nine of us – but the hard part for me would be trying to find where I could fit professionally. My work is recognised here, so I want to stay and see where that goes. In Tonga information technology is an industry that's only just starting and they're still only learning the basics. I'm interested in exploring the psychology of learning with regard to new technologies, so professionally I'm better off here. The University of South Australia has just awarded me a scholarship to finish my PhD, and in August this year I've been invited to speak in a workshop at the University of Michigan. I wouldn't have that kind of exposure in Tonga. Not only do I have the technological infrastructure here, there's a level of academic dialogue that I would miss if I went back.

I helped set up the Tongan Association in 1996. The four of us – all Tongans – were basically pioneers here in Adelaide. We wanted to use our experiences to show Tongan migrants that there are ways and means of doing things, that you don't have to face too much of a culture shock like we did. I'm the public officer now, getting the group more exposure, and saying, 'Hello! We're here, we have a dancing group and we're proud of our culture and our identity.' Also, if our kids want to identify with the Tongan culture, we show them the dances, the sort of food they used to have and tell them our stories. We take them camping and tell them how the ancestors interpreted the weather by the stars. We're showing our children, who are growing up in a multicultural society, that it's all right to stand up and say, 'I'm proud to be Tongan as well as Australian.' The association, which is more family-oriented these days, tries to help our children establish a space, an identity where they feel comfortable being in an Australian multicultural environment.

I think these are exciting times. Australians are more flexible, more accepting, and there are not that many barriers between people any more. Australia is about diverse people from multicultural backgrounds, not just pure Anglo-Saxons. Generally speaking, people have realised that the world is made up of different people and we have to learn to live together.

In the last twenty-three years I've experienced a whole transitional, attitudinal change. People are looking more at living with each other as humans, rather than saying, 'You're Tongan, I'm Australian, therefore I don't speak to Tongans.' In the next twenty-three years it won't really matter what your origins are or what you look like – it'll matter to you in terms of your identity – rather it'll be the quality of the people you interact with regardless of ethnicity. I really want to see that happen.

VILI MILISITS

Fleeing Hungary with his family in 1956, Vili Milisits spent three years in refugee camps before arriving in Australia at the age of eleven. He left school at fourteen to become an apprentice pastry chef and at the age of nineteen started his own business despite being too young to receive finance from banks. He and his wife, Rosemary, have expanded the business from just cakes and are now renowned for their great pies, pasties and sausage rolls. Vili exports to Europe and Asia, and has developed halal meat pies for the global Muslim community. The business employs over 200 people, with established bakeries in three states, plus the popular Cafe de Vili's in Adelaide.

A:1

ADELAIDE

SOUTH

AUSTRALIA

WEST

MAP REF: 199

I was eight when the Russians invaded Hungary. My father was pro-active against the Communists, so he was definitely going to be in trouble. My mother was Austrian – you could almost see her village across the border – and because we lived only about half an hour from the frontier, we ended up crossing with whatever we could carry. We left everything behind, including my alsatian. One of my oldest memories of Hungary is leaving that dog. I had to chain him up and leave him.

Eighteen months later we gained passage to Australia – this was after applying to about seven different countries – and my father just said, 'We're going.' We'd never heard of the place. In America we had relatives, in Australia we had nobody. The reason my parents chose Australia was the fact that we were already long-term refugees and here we'd be taken almost immediately, whereas America took about two years. My parents liked the fact that it was one continent. One island, with no borders. We were sick of borders.

We landed at Port Melbourne. That same evening we were put on a train to South Australia. It was a stinking hot January day when we arrived, and I had this original duffle coat – it had been cold in England – which was the height of fashion at the time. The kids in Adelaide thought that coat was fantastic. Something else I remember liking when we arrived was the bottle exchange. You could exchange a soft drink bottle for an ice-cream. Back in Hungary, when I wanted to buy an ice-cream and didn't have any money, I traded eggs. It seemed the same barter system no matter where you went.

I left school at fourteen. Maybe I was one of the kids who wanted to stay but we didn't have those choices. My father had become ill. I was apprenticed to a gentleman called Kazmer Ujvari. He's still in business. He'd be about seventy-eight now. He was a hard taskmaster, but there's no grievances. I think I was about his eleventh apprentice, the only one who ever stayed. Perhaps I was a little more mature than most kids that age. If you spend eighteen months in refugee camps, you tend to grow up fast because you have to. I'd seen the best and the worst of human behaviour. People fighting over a loaf of bread because they wouldn't share and, conversely, a slice divided between three or four people. I'd had a hell of an education by the time I came here.

I started my own business in 1967. I was nineteen. I leased some equipment and had to pay it off in a year – it was hard. I was told I was too young, that I was a snotty-nosed kid in business. I'd have people looking over the premises, saying, 'Where's your father?' Nobody would lend me any money because I was a minor. In the first year I had to go to a Japanese finance company for assistance. The Australian stuffed shirts, the banks, wouldn't listen and knocked me back, so I paid the interest – twenty-six per cent until I turned twenty-one. Meanwhile, I got married. I told my wife, 'We're going to be very poor for a few years.' For a while there we only just made ends meet.

I started out making continental cakes. Ten years into the business my sister came to me – she had a cafe in town – and said, 'Vili, I'm buying your cakes and the opposition's pies and pasties. What's wrong with you? Can't you make a pie or pasty?' We looked into it. I didn't like traditional Aussie pies, they've got mutton in them. Czechs, Poles, Germans, Russians and Hungarians hate mutton with a vengeance. If you want to insult your neighbour in Hungary you invite them around for a meal of mutton. They won't come back. I introduced steak-and-mushroom, goulash, chicken, beef rendang, chicken satay. There's no limit to what can be put in a pastry shell! Now we export to England, Germany, Italy. Today was our first order to Italy. Kangaroo pies to Italy, vegetarian pies to Italy, steak-and-mushroom pies to Italy. Germany is much the same, and I've had inquiries from Spain.

Poverty and hunger motivated me originally. I didn't like either. One thing's certain – I'll never be hungry again! I've got over a million pies in the freezers right now. If you ever go to a migrant family's place, and they invite you to eat, there'll be an abundance of food. It was very important to most immigrants that when you came to their place you could eat your fill, and that they appeared prosperous. My understanding of some other cultures is that it's not so much the house or the food but more the car they drive. Different priorities. Not in our wildest dreams when we came to Australia did we ever think that we'd own a car. It was something so remote, you wouldn't even think about it. Even when my parents built their house in Campbelltown, they didn't make a driveway. One of my brothers, he built a house with a driveway and we thought he was crazy. So, what seemed common for an Australian – an everyday event – for us was enormous wealth. Wealth that meant you could eat to your heart's content, have a job, and aspire to make your life better, to do whatever you wished in life and never be hungry or poor again.

Every pie I send overseas has got a map of Australia on it. My picture of this country is an aerial shot of the outback – twenty-five square miles – and underneath the phrase: 'Cattle 25, humans 0, pollution 0!' We were at a Variety Club bash in the middle of the desert – no-man's land, middle of the night – and this lone, Japanese push-bike rider comes over the horizon. We had a refrigerated van with a microwave, so we pulled up and said, 'You hungry, mate?' We fed him pies, gave him a Vili's shirt and hat, and asked him if he was lonely out there. You know what he said? 'How can I be lonely? Look at all those stars.' We take all that for granted. When I go bush, I never sleep in a motel. I take a swag, leave it open and watch the stars.